HST

From 1990 to the Present Day

MARK V. PIKE

BRITAIN'S RAILWAYS SERIES, VOLUME 33

Front cover image: A fabulous summer's day sees 43357 (formerly 43157) approaching Whiteball Tunnel, between Exeter and Taunton, with a Plymouth to Edinburgh service. 26 June 2010.

Back cover image: It is a far cry from the Grand Central livery previously carried by these examples! A view of Rail Adventure 43468 (with 43465) at Fareham, waiting to work back to Eastleigh after a test run. 29 March 2022.

Title page image: Ex-East Midlands Trains 43274, in purple livery, has since gained Colas Rail logos on the bodysides and is used on test trains. It is seen here on the rear of 1Q23, the 05.56 Reading to Salisbury (via Yeovil Junction/Exeter St Davids) at Gillingham (Dorset) on its return from Exeter. 18 November 2021.

Contents page image: Virgin CrossCountry 43156 raving through Dawlish Warren with a service bound for Penzance. 16 August 2002.

Published by Key Books
An imprint of Key Publishing Ltd
PO Box 100
Stamford
Lincs PE19 1XQ

www.keypublishing.com

The right of Mark V. Pike to be identified as the author of this book has been asserted in accordance with the Copyright, Designs and Patents Act 1988 Sections 77 and 78.

Copyright © Mark V. Pike, 2022

ISBN 978 1 80282 249 6

Typeset by SJmagic DESIGN SERVICES, India.

Contents

Introduction

Quite a few operators have used High Speed Trains (HSTs) over the years, including East Coast, Midland Main Line and Virgin CrossCountry. So, after my first volume *HSTs: The Western Region*, I have been trawling through my archive of images collected over the years and I realised I would be able to produce a further volume of the HSTs at work on other regions and areas of the UK. Many of these are from more recent years but with a few older images among them.

As a result of the mass withdrawal of 2018–19 when their successors, in the form of the Hitachi bi-mode Class 800/801/802 units, came on stream, many power cars were put into storage. Some have since gone on to be scrapped altogether. Fortunately, not everyone deemed them life expired.

Some smaller operators have been looking closely at their potential in recent times and TOCs including Colas Rail and Locomotive Services have actually now acquired some examples for further use. The Colas Rail ones are now being used on test trains operated for Network Rail, while Locomotive Services has two dedicated charter sets that are used UK-wide, utilising four power cars with a few as spares. While it is pretty obvious that not all will be saved, I do hope further use for some of the stored ones can be found. If not, they will just gradually rust away and become of no use to anyone.

Arriva CrossCountry 43366 and 43384 passing on diverted services to and from Plymouth at Bradford-on-Avon. 16 March 2019.

Chapter 1

East Coast Main Line

The HSTs were first introduced to the East Coast Main Line (ECML) in the late 1970s as a replacement for the Class 55 'Deltic' locos that had in turn replaced steam in the early 1960s. Although electrification came to the line in the late 1980s, and despite changing liveries and various operators over the years, HSTs were still regularly used right up to the end of 2019, working alongside the Class 91 electric locos. This section illustrates a few workings, mainly in more recent years, and also some views of East Coast sets operating away from their normal route.

The first image shows the last-built power car 43198 in ex-works condition as it departs Doncaster on the rear of a King's Cross-bound service. This power car is still in service today, working for GWR on Castle services and, very unusually, carrying two separate names on each bodyside: *Driver Brian Cooper 15 June 1947-5 October 1999* and *Driver Stan Martin 25 June 1950-6 November 2004*. 1985.

In a rare experimental livery variation of a full yellow end and a white cab roof, this is 43038 *National Railway Museum, The First 10 Years 1975-1985* arriving at King's Cross. This livery was deemed to be of no advantage and the power car was later repainted in the standard style. Later re-engined and renumbered as 43238, it is currently stored at Ely Papworth sidings with a seemingly rather bleak future. 25 August 1993.

This is 43105 *Hartlepool* ticking over at King's Cross while the set is cleaned and watered in readiness for its next journey north. Later renumbered 43305, this is another example now stored at Ely Papworth awaiting its fate. 25 August 1993.

Another view at King's Cross as 43106 *Songs of Praise* arrives with a train from the north. Later to become 43306, the power car is also now in storage at Ely Papworth. 26 May 1993.

The first of three views of the changing appearance of 43039 over the years. In Great North Eastern Railway (GNER) livery, this is the power car standing at Aberdeen after arrival from King's Cross. 28 February 2000.

Soon after being re-engined and outshopped in National Express livery, this is a rare view of the power car carrying its original number. Upon refurbishment and re-engineering, most East Coast power cars were renumbered in the 432xx or 433xx series but this one managed to escape for a few days and carry its original number! Brightening up a very dull day, it is seen in spotless condition departing York with an Aberdeen to King's Cross service. 22 February 2008.

Another 11 years on and we see the now correctly numbered 43239, since painted in London North Eastern Railway (LNER) livery, racing through Doncaster with a King's Cross-bound service. Since ending its career with LNER, and after a quick repaint at Eastleigh Works, the power car is now in service with Arriva CrossCountry. 12 February 2019.

Still at Doncaster, this is long time East Coast allocated 43095 *Perth* approaching with a nine-coach King's Cross to Aberdeen service. Later renumbered 43295, it is currently stored at Ely Papworth. 30 December 2003.

With a tiny vinyl name near the radiator grille on the white band, 43095 *Perth* is seen again in a hybrid GNER/National Express livery, this time under the magnificent overall roof at York with a King's Cross to Aberdeen service. 22 February 2008.

Yet another hybrid livery as we see a refurbished and renumbered but now un-named 43295 passing Doncaster at speed with 1E03, the 06.26 Edinburgh to King's Cross service. This power car is now one of the large collection stored at Ely. 23 September 2015.

Standing at Inverness, this is 43096 *The Great Racer* after arriving with the 'Highland Chieftain' service from King's Cross. 28 February 2000.

Now renumbered as 43296 and un-named, the power car is seen passing Alexandra Palace with 1S16, the 12.00 King's Cross to Inverness 'Highland Chieftain'. After withdrawal from service by LNER, this particular power car was taken on by Rail Adventure as a source of spares for its other examples. It is currently at Eastleigh Works. 13 November 2018.

This time we see 43108 *Old Course St Andrews* at York about to depart with 1S16, the 12.00 London King's Cross to Inverness 'Highland Chieftain' service once again. As 43308, this power car actually carried the name *Highland Chieftain* in later years but is now another example acquired by Rail Adventure as a source of spares at Eastleigh Works. 22 February 2008.

City of Inverness

During 2006–07, Virgin CrossCountry found that its 'Voyager' units were not suited to some of the busy West Country services and became hopelessly overcrowded, so a hired-in GNER set was used alongside its own HST sets, mostly on summer Saturdays in an attempt to ease the situation. In absolutely foul weather, 43105 *City of Inverness* looks a little out of place as it waits for departure from Exeter St Davids with 1E46, the 10.32 Paignton to Newcastle. Later numbered 43305, this power car is now amongst the large number stored at Ely Papworth. 2 September 2006.

Back in usual territory now as we see 43111 *Scone Palace* arriving at a cold Aberdeen with a service from King's Cross. Later renumbered 43311, it is now in storage at Ely. 3 February 2004.

Scone Palace

This is 43119 *Harrogate Spa* passing The Sidings Hotel (well-known amongst rail enthusiasts) at Shipton-by-Beningbrough, a few miles north of York, with a service for King's Cross. Later to become 43319, it is now stored at Ely Papworth. 22 February 2008.

Back to York station for this image of 43110 *Stirlingshire* in a hybrid GNER/National Express livery, departing with an Aberdeen to King's Cross service. 22 February 2008.

Now in LNER livery and numbered 43310, the same power car seen in the previous image is nearing the end of its active service on the rear of a northbound service departing Doncaster. Almost needless to say, this one is now stored at Ely Papworth. 12 February 2019.

Harrogate Spa

43119 *Harrogate Spa* is seen again, this time departing York with a southbound service for King's Cross. 20 February 2008.

Now transformed into 43319 and wearing LNER livery, the same power car is seen at York once again but this time bringing up the rear of an Aberdeen to King's Cross service. The power car is now stored at Ely Papworth. 23 September 2019.

Specially prepared for its naming ceremony, this is 43238 approaching Doncaster with 1N81, the 09.08 King's Cross to York. 23 September 2015.

A close-up view of 43238 *National Railway Museum 40 Years 1975-2015* during its re-dedication ceremony at York station. Despite all the hard work to make the power car look like this, it was erased when it was painted all over red and went to work briefly for East Midlands Railway. It is currently dumped at Ely Papworth. Compare this image to the second picture in this book taken 21 years earlier. 23 September 2015.

The route to the West Country has always been very popular and busy, especially during the summer months. Arriva franchise CrossCountry soon came to realise this when it gained the operation from Virgin in November 2007 and found that more capacity was needed. Due to this, a spare National Express set was hired in on various summer Saturdays in 2008 to ease the situation. On a rather gloomy day, this is 43317 during the livery transition period from GNER to National Express in ex-works condition passing Powderham, near Starcross, with 1V29, the 07.25 Manchester Piccadilly to Newquay service. It has since become another power car stored at Ely Papworth. 30 August 2008.

On the rear of the train in the previous shot going down to Newquay was 43053 in a hybrid National Express/GNER livery. With the gloomy weather only having got worse, this is the return 1M28, the 15.22 Newquay to Manchester Piccadilly, passing Aller on the approach to Newton Abbott. Even this location has changed out of all recognition, with the removal of the bridge the image was taken from and a new by-pass having been constructed to the left of the picture. This power car went on to work for First Great Western (FGW)/Great Western Railway (GWR) sometime after this date but, unfortunately, it has now become one of only a few (so far) to have been cut up. 30 August 2008.

Some 11 years on and CrossCountry was still hiring in an East Coast set on summer-dated trains to the west. This is the strange and colourful sight of a full LNER set passing along Marine Parade at Dawlish headed by 43257 *Bounds Green* with 43251 on the rear of 1V46, the 06.45 York to Plymouth. 43257 is now operating with Colas Rail and is used on various test trains across the UK. 24 August 2019.

A fine late summer's day has brought out the visitors to the beach as we see 43251 on the return service of the train in the previous picture, 1S53, the 13.26 Plymouth to Edinburgh, passing through Dawlish. This is another power car since taken on by Colas Rail for test train use. 24 August 2019.

Hired in by LNER, this is East Midlands Trains (EMT) 43061 passing Alexandra Palace with 1Y11, the 06.30 Newcastle to King's Cross. This is another one of the few examples that have since been scrapped. 13 November 2018.

With the follow up working of the train in the last image, this is EMT-liveried 43075 approaching Alexandra Palace with 1D11, the 11.03 London King's Cross to Leeds service. This is another of the power cars that have now been scrapped. 13 November 2018.

Under the fine overall roof at York, and with another of those ridiculously tiny vinyl names on the white stripe, this is 43206 *Kingdom of Fife* (formerly 43006) bringing up the rear of 1E13, the 07.55 Inverness to King's Cross 'Highland Chieftain' service. This is yet another example currently stored at Ely Papworth. 21 February 2008.

A decade later and now un-named, 43206 is captured passing Alexandra Palace with 1D13, the 12.03 King's Cross to Leeds service. 13 November 2018.

There have been so many livery variations down the years to most of these power cars, it is quite difficult to keep up with them all! This is 43302 (formerly 43102) in overall East Coast light grey awaiting departure north from King's Cross. This power car is down in the record books as the world's fastest diesel locomotive, which (along with 43159) achieved 148.5mph back in 1987 between York and Northallerton. In recognition of this, it was returned to InterCity livery and donated to the National Railway Museum upon withdrawal by East Midlands Railway (EMR). It is currently, as of April 2022, on display at the Locomotion Museum at Shildon. 23 July 2014.

During the GNER/National Express transition days, 43306 arrives at York with a terminating service from King's Cross. This power car is currently stored at Ely Papworth. 20 February 2008.

Now in a hybrid National Express/Virgin livery, this is another view of 43306 approaching York, this time from the north with an Aberdeen to King's Cross service. 23 September 2015.

This is 43208 *Lincolnshire Echo* (formerly 43008) arriving at Doncaster with a northbound service, which is unusually made up of nine coaches. After displacement from LNER, this example was taken on by CrossCountry. 12 February 2019.

43299 (formerly 43099) is seen on the same day as the last shot at Doncaster, racing through with a northbound service. After withdrawal from passenger service, this power car has joined the small Network Rail fleet for use on the New Measurement Train (NMT). 12 February 2019.

This time we see 43320 (formerly 43120) and set in former National Express but East Coast branded colours waiting to depart York with a northbound service from King's Cross. This is another of the unlucky examples that now finds itself in storage at Ely Papworth. 18 August 2012.

Just three years later, 43320 is seen again at York now in full Virgin livery, departing from the same platform as the last image with the 10.00 King's Cross to Aberdeen service. 23 September 2015.

Still at York, we see 43317 (formerly 43117) having just arrived with the 10.00 King's Cross to Aberdeen, while to the right is West Coast Railway's (WCR) 47804 on the 'Royal Scotsman' charter train. 43317 is now amongst the collection dumped at Ely Papworth. 23 September 2015.

Chapter 2

Midland Main Line

The Midland Main Line (MML) was the last of the major routes to see HSTs, first receiving an allocation back in the early 1980s when they replaced the well liked Class 45 'Peak' locomotives. Following this, they were the mainstay of services to and from London St Pancras to Leicester, Nottingham, Derby and Sheffield until new Class 222s were introduced in the mid-2000s. Similar to the ECML, the HSTs worked alongside the new units right up until 2020. This section shows a few MML workings, mainly in later years, but also depicts a few sets off route away from their normal working areas.

Waiting to depart from Derby with a service for London St Pancras is 43045 in the attractive green and teal livery it carried during the late 1990s and early 2000s. Although this power car was briefly taken on by Colas Rail in 2021, it is currently in storage at Long Marston with an uncertain future. 23 June 2001.

Derby again and this time we see 43046 *Royal Philharmonic* having just arrived from St Pancras. This power car has more recently come under the ownership of Locomotive Services and operates throughout the UK on its revived Blue Pullman charter set; an image of this can been seen towards the end of this book. 23 June 2001.

This time we see 43052 receiving a screen wash at Leicester as it pauses with a London St Pancras to Nottingham service. Some 22 years after this image was taken, this example is now coincidentally stored at Leicester. 29 May 2000.

This is the first of four images of long MML-allocated 43049 *Neville Hill*. It is seen calling at Chesterfield with a St Pancras to Nottingham service. 17 September 1991.

Showing off the Midland Mainline livery to good effect, 43049 is this time awaiting departure from London St Pancras with a Nottingham train. The gas holders were a well-known landmark here. 3 April 1997.

Nine years later and 43049 is in a much less colourful Midland Mainline livery at a dull Exeter St Davids of all places while heading the set hired in for 1V29, the 07.25 Leeds to Plymouth service. 22 February 2006.

A further ten years on and towards the end of its career on the MML, 43049 is seen passing Sileby with 1D22, the 10.15 St Pancras to Nottingham. This was not the end for 43049 however, see the last section of this book for how it looks now! 12 February 2016.

Pulling away from East Midlands Parkway is 43047 with 1B53, the 14.32 Nottingham to London St Pancras. This is another power car currently with Locomotive Services but has yet to be returned to use. 12 February 2016.

Another long-term MML power car was 43050, seen at Leicester on the rear of a London-bound service. This power car more recently saw use on overhead electrification test trains with Data Acquisition and Testing Services (DATS) and is currently stored at the former Brush Traction works at Loughborough. 3 February 2016.

This is 43052 powering past Sileby with 1B38, the 11.32 Nottingham to London St Pancras service. 12 February 2016.

With just over two years to go until the removal of HSTs from MML services, this is 43058 at Nottingham awaiting departure with the 15.45 service to London. Upon withdrawal from these services, it was far from the end for this example though. It was taken on by Locomotive Services and, along with 43059, painted into a green livery with a silver stripe during 2021 for use by Rail Charter Services. See the section at the end of this volume. 13 February 2019.

With a former LNER buffet coach in the consist, braking for the stop at Leicester is 43083 with 1B53, the 14.32 Nottingham to St Pancras. This power car was also taken on by Locomotive Services but is currently at Eastleigh Works being used as a source of spares. 3 February 2016.

Left: 43054 approaches Sileby with 1B28, the 09.32 Nottingham to St Pancras. This is another power car currently under the control of DATS. 12 February 2016.

Below: Bringing up the rear of the train in the previous image is 43076 *In Support of Help For Heroes*. This example is currently in storage for DATS at the former Brush Works at Loughborough. 12 February 2016.

43052 is seen again, this time arriving at Leicester with 1B48, the 13.32 Nottingham to London St Pancras service. 3 February 2016.

Also just arrived at Leicester is 43082 *Railway Children, The Voice for Street Children Worldwide* with 1D21, the 09.05 St Pancras to Nottingham. This is one of the lucky few that have so far been preserved, being purchased by 125 Heritage Ltd during 2021 and is now at the Colne Valley Railway. 3 February 2016.

This is 43054 again, this time at Nottingham awaiting departure with 1B98, the 16.12 Nottingham to St Pancras. 11 February 2016.

Left: 43048 *T.C.B. Miller MBE* approaches Leicester with 1B28, the 09.32 Nottingham to St Pancras. This is another power car lucky enough to be preserved, this time by the 125 Group. 3 February 2016.

Below: Bringing up the rear of the train in the previous photo, this is 43046 at Leicester. This power car has now found further work with Locomotive Services on its Blue Pullman charter set. 3 February 2016.

Catching a nice patch of low winter sunshine, 43059 brings up the rear of 1D43, the 13.35 St Pancras to Nottingham. This is another example now with Locomotive Services, mainly for use on the 'Staycation' green-liveried set. 3 February 2016.

Right: Slowing for the stop at Leicester, this is 43073 with 1B34, the 10.32 Nottingham to St Pancras. This is another lucky example that has been preserved by 125 Heritage and is currently located at the Colne Valley Railway. 3 February 2016.

Below: This is 43081 approaching Sileby with 1D32, the 12.15 London to Nottingham. This is yet another preserved example, this time located at the Crewe Heritage Centre. 12 February 2016.

The next few shots show hired-in MML sets in use on CrossCountry services. Allocated to the Western Region when new, 43178 went on to have a varied allocation. It is seen during its days with Midland Mainline but on hire to Virgin CrossCountry and back on the Western approaching Westbury with 1V29, the 07.25 Leeds to Plymouth. On this particular day, CrossCountry services were being diverted via Westbury due to engineering work. The power car has since been refurbished and is currently actually operating for CrossCountry (Arriva) as 43378. I hope you kept up there? 23 November 2006.

This time we see 43066 with 1E47, the 11.45 Plymouth to Newcastle at Bristol Temple Meads. Currently operated by DATS, this power car most recently saw passenger use at the Chinnor diesel gala in April 2022. 28 September 2006.

43056 is seen on the rear of the train in the last picture at Bristol Temple Meads. A few years after this date, 43056 was transferred to FGW/GWR and soon after withdrawal by that TOC, it was donated to the Welsh Railways Trust during 2021. It is now located at the Gwili Railway. 28 September 2006.

Departing a very damp Exeter St Davids, this is 43044 leading 1V29, the 07.25 Leeds to Plymouth service. This is another example preserved by the 125 Group during 2021. 2 September 2006.

Making an interesting comparison with FGW examples 43030 and 43138 in the distance, this is 43058 at Bristol Temple Meads on the rear of 1E47, the 11.45 Plymouth to Newcastle service. Along with 43059, this power car now operates for Locomotive Services, mainly on its 'Staycation' set. 12 October 2006.

Yet another damp day, this is 43060 seen at Taunton with 1V29, the 07.25 Leeds to Plymouth service. After seeing a short period of use with Colas Rail, this power car is currently in storage at Long Marston. 6 October 2006.

43043 is seen arriving at Bristol Temple Meads with 1E47, the 11.45 Plymouth to Newcastle service. This one is also currently in storage at Long Marston. 12 October 2006.

To finish this section, here is a what might have been! 43064 is seen in the heart of the New Forest National Park, just south of Beaulieu Road station, leading 1Z43, the 06.13 Sheffield to Swanage. This was 'The Swanage Samaritan' charter organised by East Midlands Trains, complete with temporary South West Trains branding on the power car and first few coaches. It was rumoured at the time that when MML finished with its HSTs that some (or all) would transfer to South West Trains for use on Waterloo to Exeter services, but unfortunately nothing ever came of this. This is the only HST to date that has ever visited Swanage, although, a few years earlier, a FGW set did get as far as Corfe Castle but terminated there due to some sort of gauging problem. This power car is currently stored at Long Marston. The old concrete permanent way hut was made especially for the Southern Railway back in the 1930s at the Exmouth Junction concrete works, near Exeter, and it is amazing still in situ! 14 June 2014.

This is 43089 on the rear of the train as it passed by. This power car was used to test lithium-ion battery hybrid traction technology during the mid-2000s in conjunction with the NMT, again without any further developments happening. Upon withdrawal from front line service, it was purchased by the 125 Group. 14 June 2014.

Chapter 3
Cross Country

H ST sets were first used on cross-country routes during the early 1980s, at the time working alongside trains hauled by Class 47 locos. In January 1997, Virgin Trains took over the whole sphere of inter-regional services, becoming Virgin CrossCountry (Virgin XC) with sets still working services in conjunction with the loco-hauled trains up until 2002. This brought about an interesting period in the late 1990s when a livery change from InterCity to the bright red Virgin colours meant both could be seen together. This section depicts the run up to the changeover and also shows the sets in the eye-catching Virgin livery during the late 1990s up until the end of Virgin XC in 2007.

Above: With its distinctive large white nameplate, this is 43193 *Plymouth – City of Discovery* departing Didcot Parkway with a Bournemouth to Edinburgh service as a FGW set departs in the opposite direction heading for Paddington. This power car ended its main line service with GWR but is currently stored at Plymouth Laira depot as a source of spares. 12 May 2001.

Left: In the early style Virgin XC livery, this is 43153 *The English Riviera Torquay– Paignton–Brixham* arriving at Bristol Temple Meads with a northbound service from Plymouth. This one is now working for GWR on its Castle services and carries the name *Chûn Castle*. 19 July 1997.

Also in the early Virgin XC livery, this is buffer-fitted 43068 *The Red Nose* waiting to depart west from Bristol Temple Meads. Since refurbished and renumbered as 43468, the power car is now owned by Rail Adventure and is currently at Eastleigh Works. Incidentally, the nameplate it carried in this image was sold at auction in 2017 for an amazing £960! 19 July 1997.

In what was then standard Virgin livery, 43158 *Dartmoor The Pony Express* is seen passing Starcross with a northbound service. This power car is still in traffic today operating for GWR and named *Kingswear Castle*. 9 August 2001.

Looking in the other direction at Starcross, this is 43091 approaching with a Penzance-bound service. This example was later used by FGW/GWR and is currently stored at Laira depot. 9 August 2001.

Moving now to Bournemouth, 43062 is arriving with a service for Poole. After working for some years on inter-regional services and later with Virgin XC, it was taken on by Network Rail and is now painted in bright yellow livery, carrying the name *John Armitt* and used throughout the UK on its NMT. See the section on Network Rail later in the book. 12 September 1992.

43070 is seen arriving at Basingstoke with a Poole to Edinburgh service. Another power car that worked quite a few years on cross-country services, it ended its main line service with GWR and was disposed of to Sims Metals at Newport Docks in January 2022. 25 November 1992.

Still at Basingstoke, this is buffer-fitted 43014 about to depart south with a service bound for Poole. This example had a similar later life to 43062 mentioned earlier. It is now in yellow livery as part of the small Network Rail fleet and used UK-wide on the NMT, it has also been named rather appropriately *The Railway Observer*. 10 July 1992.

A little further south, we see 43116 *City of Kingston Upon Hull* waiting to depart south with a Poole-bound service. This was the second power car (the first being 43113) to receive cast nameplates way back in May 1983; it was however de-named for a while in the late 1980s/early 1990s but later received the replacement aluminium plates it carries here. In more recent years, it was numbered 43316 and is now in storage at Ely Papworth. 11 February 1992.

Two views now of 43100. This one shows it on the rear of a Glasgow/Edinburgh to Poole service awaiting departure time at Crewe. It is carrying the aluminium nameplates *Craigentinny*, a name it first received back in 1984 as cast plates. 7 April 1993.

Craigentinny

Seen here calling at Newport during the short time HSTs were used on Virgin XC services to South Wales, this is 43100 now in red livery and carrying the vinyl name *Blackpool Rock*. In later years, the power car was used on ECML services carrying the number 43300 and re-named back as *Craigentinny* with cast plates once again. 5 May 1999.

During the late 1980s and early 1990s, Bournemouth was a good place to see cross-country services utilising HSTs. This is 43093 *Lady in Red* on the rear of a northbound service, while to the right is 43196 *The Newspaper Society Founded 1836* which had just arrived from the north. Both of these power cars are now with GWR but, although 43093 is still in service, 43196 is currently stored at Plymouth Laira. 26 May 2001.

Another one of the few examples that were fitted with buffers during the late 1980s, this is 43068 speeding through Eastleigh with a service for Poole. This power car has since been renumbered 43468 and is now with Rail Adventure. 29 May 1992.

Making the call at Southampton Central, 43071 is seen on the rear of a Poole to Edinburgh service. Later to receive the name *Forward Birmingham* and more recently working for GWR, this example has now been preserved by 125 Heritage and is located at the Colne Valley Railway. 30 October 1991.

On a hot summer's day, this is 43045 *The Grammar School Doncaster AD 1350* at Birmingham New Street with 1S03, the 08.40 Poole to Edinburgh 'Wessex Scot' service. This power car was transferred to MML services sometime after this date but is now currently in storage at Long Marston. 10 July 1992.

A short-lived train that operated during the mid-1990s was the 07.37 Manchester Piccadilly to London Waterloo, which provided a connection with Eurostar services. The train is seen passing Kensington Olympia with 43099 at the helm. This example was withdrawn from ECML services as 43299 during 2019 but was taken on by Network Rail soon afterwards and now sees use on test trains across the UK. 4 June 1996.

This is 43094 racing through Totnes with a service for Penzance. Upon displacement from Virgin XC, this power car was stored for a while until it was taken on by FGW and is still in service today with GWR, carrying the name *St Mawes Castle*. 30 July 2002.

This is 43094 again, this time in storage at the very unlikely location of Minehead on the West Somerset Railway heritage line! It was only here a while until being taken on by FGW and put back into main line service. 30 September 2005.

It is hard to believe but even this shot is not now possible, regardless of the sort of train passing! The whole section of sea wall here opposite Marine Parade at Dawlish was totally rebuilt during the early 2020s and that has raised the height of the wall, with a fence on top of that making photography difficult. 43089 passes with a northbound service. Thankfully this power car has since been preserved by the 125 Group. 21 July 2001.

Back to the early days of the use of HSTs on cross-country services, this is the first of two images of 43160 at Poole for its naming ceremony. This shot sees the immaculate power car arriving from the sidings into the up platform. 27 April 1991.

The driver hops out of the cab of 43160 as the short ceremony is underway to reveal the reflective metal nameplate *Storm Force* to celebrate the Children's Club (Storm Force) of the RNLI, which is based at Poole. It also marked the introduction of HSTs on inter-regional services to/from Poole. The set then formed a service to the north. 27 April 1991.

With just five Mk.3s in tow, 43079 is bearing down on the station at Eastleigh during the last months of Virgin XC HST use with a service bound for Bournemouth. After being withdrawn from service with GWR in the late 2010s, this example was sent for scrap at Newport in January 2022.

Another five-coach set is seen heading north at Eastleigh, with last-built 43198 *HMS Penzance* leading the way. This power car is still in use with GWR at the time of writing and is unusual in carrying two names, on one side it is *Driver Brian Cooper 15 June 1947-5 October 1999* and on the other it is *Driver Stan Martin 25 June 1950-6 November 2004*, two drivers that were tragically killed in separate accidents on the former Western Region. 11 April 2003.

As far southwest as you can travel by train, this is 43008 at Penzance station on the rear of a service for the north. This power car more recently operated with LNER carrying the number 43208 and is now in use with the Arriva-owned CrossCountry franchise. 15 January 2000.

43098 *The Railway Children* is captured passing the signal box and semaphore signals as it heads south through Lostwithiel with a Glasgow to Penzance service. This example is now in service with GWR and renamed *Walton Castle*. 30 August 2002.

Looking in the other direction, this is 43184 opening up as it passes Lostwithiel with a northbound service from Penzance. A former Western Region example, later going on to become 43384, it is now in regular service with Arriva CrossCountry. 30 August 2002.

This is another of those short-formed sets that could often be seen in the last months of Virgin XC service. 43196 *The Newspaper Society* draws to a halt at Exeter St Davids with a Plymouth-bound service. Although now the responsibility of GWR, 43196 is currently stored at Plymouth Laira as a source of spares. 1 February 2003.

Still at Exeter St Davids, but some time before the creation of Virgin XC, this is 43121 *West Yorkshire Metropolitan County* arriving from the west with a service for the north of England. This power car has actually managed to stay on cross-country services and, after refurbishment and the fitment of an MTU engine, now operates with CrossCountry to the present day with the running number 43321. 15 June 1993.

Right: The late 1990s saw a transition from InterCity livery to the eye-catching Virgin red and mixed formations were common. This is 43070 awaiting departure from Exeter St Davids with a service for Edinburgh. 23 August 1997.

Below: We now head to the South Western Main Line for these two views of a Bournemouth to Manchester Piccadilly service approaching Micheldever. Viewed to the south, this is 43086 leading a five-coach set. This is another power car currently stored at Laira. 15 April 2003.

On the rear of the same train was 43197 *The Railway Magazine*. The small station of Micheldever can be seen in the distance, as can the chalk cutting on the approach to the twin Popham Tunnels further distant still. Originally carrying the name *Railway Magazine Centenary 1897-1997*, these nameplates were removed some time in 2000 and this shortened version attached soon after. However, the plates it is seen carrying in this image are now carried by Freightliner's 66503. 43197 itself is currently stored at Plymouth. 15 April 2003.

Back in the South West again, the huge nameplate reveals that this is 43092 *Institution of Mechanical Engineers 150th Anniversary 1847-1997* captured passing the well-known location of the dry Cockwood Harbour, near Starcross. Most photographers know how tricky it can be to get a shot with the tide in! 15 August 2002.

43196 *The Newspaper Society* is seen about to pass beneath Coastguards Footbridge and approaching Dawlish station with a service for Penzance. This power car is currently stored at Laira. 8 August 2001.

Right: The footbridge mentioned in the previous image is above and to the rear of the train as we see 43099 passing Dawlish station with a Plymouth service. The unusual signal box seen to the left was at the time listed. However, it was to stand in an increasingly decrepit state for another 11 years after the date of this image when it was decided to de-list it and demolish it. A rather sad end for a distinctive structure. Now renumbered 43299, this power car is now operating for Network Rail. 4 August 2001.

Below: A lone person braves the wind, rain and cold of a winter's day as 43193 *Plymouth Spirit of Discovery* passes by on the rear of a northbound service at Dawlish. This is yet another one of the large collection stored at Plymouth. 1 February 2002.

Above: Buffer-fitted 43084 *County of Derbyshire* is seen beneath the wires at Shipton by Beningborough, just north of York, with an Edinburgh bound service. After re-engineering, it was renumbered 43484, seeing use with Grand Central and EMT. It has now been taken on by Rail Adventure and even visited Germany for a brief period at the end of 2021. It has since returned back to Eastleigh Works but is yet to be used on the main line at the time of writing. 6 April 2002.

Left: This time we are on the West Coast Main Line, with 43160 approaching Tring with a Blackpool to London Euston service. This one is now in service with GWR on Castle services. 5 November 2003.

During the first year of HST operation on services to Bournemouth and Poole, 43070 makes a characteristically smoky arrival at Birmingham New Street with a Poole to Edinburgh service. 22 April 1992.

For a while during the early 1990s, a few inter-regional HST services operated as far as Weymouth on summer Saturdays. This is buffer-fitted 43080 awaiting departure from Wareham with the extended (usually starting at Poole) 'Wessex Scot' from Weymouth to Edinburgh. 7 September 1991.

Ten years later and now wearing the Virgin red livery, 43080 is seen having just arrived at Plymouth with a service from Manchester Piccadilly. This power car has a similar history to 43084, seen earlier in this section. It is now renumbered 43480, operating with Rail Adventure and was with 43484 when they were both sent to Germany for a brief period in 2021. Both are now back at Eastleigh Works awaiting their next moves. 21 July 2001.

The first of a few images from Basingstoke now as 43097 winds its way into the station with a Manchester Piccadilly to Poole service. This one went on to work with FGW and is currently working for GWR carrying the name *Castle Drogo*. 17 October 1991.

Turning the camera to the left on the same day, this is 43099 departing on the rear of a corresponding service from Poole to Manchester Piccadilly. The huge numbers carried on the front by many power cars at the time was really handy for identification at a distance! 43099 went on to work on the ECML until withdrawal during 2019 as 43299. It now operates for Network Rail on various test trains. 17 October 1991.

Here we see 43093 *York Festival '88* arriving with a service from Poole. Currently operating with GWR, the power car now carries the name *Old Oak Common HST Depot 1976-2018*, being one of the final examples to leave that depot when it closed in 2018. 10 July 1992.

This time we see 43091 arriving with a Poole-bound service. Although this one has had a similar former working life as 43093 seen in the last image, it is currently stored by GWR at Laira as a source of spares. 17 October 1991.

Our last view of Basingstoke for a while sees buffer-fitted 43067 making its scheduled call with a train from Poole for the north of England. Later in its life and renumbered as 43467, it worked for Great Central and latterly for EMT but is now with Rail Adventure stored at Eastleigh Works. 10 July 1992.

Nine years later, during its time working for Virgin XC, 43067 departs from Dawlish station with a Plymouth-bound service. 4 August 2001.

Approaching Burton upon Trent, this is 43182 with a service from Plymouth heading north. This one only worked for a relatively short time on inter-regional services and soon found its way back on to Western Region diagrams. However once dispensed with by GWR in 2019, it was repainted in Inter7City livery and is now in service north of the border with ScotRail. 26 February 1992.

This is 43070 again, this time approaching Crewe station with the southbound 'Wessex Scot' service bound for Poole. 7 April 1993.

This is 43078 *Golowan Festival Penzance* in one of the through lines at Plymouth station. It had been removed from a set earlier in the day due to a fault and FGW's 43017 has just arrived to take it to Laira depot for attention. 43078 still operates to this day for CrossCountry but now carries the number 43378 and is fitted with an MTU engine in place of its original Paxman Valenta. 1 August 2002.

Chapter 4
Arriva CrossCountry

B y the end of 2007, the contract held by Virgin Trains was up for renewal and attracted other bidders, with Arriva emerging as the winner. Amongst other changes, all CrossCountry services would now call at Birmingham New Street, and none would serve London. Most of these services would be operated using Class 220/221 'Voyagers' but there was also a commitment in this franchise to use ten power cars and 40 Mk.3 coaches.

Midland Mainline had six power cars and 14 coaches that were off lease from late 2007 that were used, and the remaining four power cars came from Virgin XC, some being ex-store and in a pretty bad state of repair! The coaches used were five ex-Virgin CrossCountry Mk.3s and 21 ex-Virgin West Coast loco-hauled Mk.3 coaches that had to be modified before use. Many of these coaches were being withdrawn from the West Coast due to the Class 390 'Pendolinos' entering service. The HST sets with Arriva are currently operated under the banner 'CrossCountry by Arriva' and this section depicts a few of their current operations.

Right: CrossCountry's first power car to be repainted in its house colours, 43301 (formerly 43101) was released from its overhaul on 16 July 2008. It is seen just over a month later heading a northbound service at Powderham, near Starcross. The stock it has in tow was a former Midland Mainline set that had yet to be repainted in CrossCountry livery. 30 August 2008.

Below: Spot the train! 43357 (formerly 43157) is engulfed by the sea as it approaches Dawlish station on an unusually wild April day with 1C22, the 09.48 Bristol Temple Meads to Plymouth service. This is the precise spot where the wall was breached just two years earlier during the powerful storm of February 2014. 10 April 2016.

At first glance there might not seem to be anything unusual about this shot of 43207 (formerly 43007) passing along the sea wall near Dawlish, but actually it is a southbound service working on the up line! On this day, there were track circuit failures in the area which resulted in only the up line being available for trains for a while. The whole section along here is bi-directionally signalled so that trains can run in either direction on both lines, not at the same time though obviously! 13 June 2012.

Left: 43357 is seen again, this time arriving at Derby with an Edinburgh to Plymouth service. 5 March 2009.

Below: On a fine early spring day at Cam & Dursley, just south of Gloucester, this is 43384 (formerly 43184) heading south with 1V50, the 06.06 Edinburgh to Plymouth. 5 March 2010.

Having just passed over the flyover at Cogload Junction, where the direct line to London Paddington via Castle Cary and Newbury diverges, this is 43303 (formerly 43103) with 1V44, the 06.11 Leeds to Plymouth service racing towards Taunton. 26 August 2011.

Right: This is 43301 pulling away from the Taunton stop with 1V44, the 06.11 Leeds to Plymouth service. The huge apartment buildings in the background were quite a recent addition at this time. 10 December 2014.

Below: The classic shot on the sea wall as 43357 approaches Sprey Point on a blustery winter's morning, soon after passing Teignmouth with 1S51, the 12.27 Plymouth to Edinburgh service. 11 February 2011.

Above: With the recent rebuilding of the sea wall at this location, this wonderful view is no longer quite the same. 43366 (formerly 43166) is heading south past Marine Parade at Dawlish with 1V44, the 06.00 Leeds to Plymouth service. 28 August 2015.

Left: An unusual perspective of Dawlish station this time as 43285 (formerly 43085) approaches with a late running 1S51, the 12.27 Plymouth to Edinburgh service. 16 August 2018.

One of the two latest additions to the fleet by CrossCountry, this is 43239 (formerly 43039) that was in use with LNER on ECML services up until late 2019. It is recorded at Bristol Temple Meads on the rear of 1V44, the 06.11 Leeds to Plymouth service. 13 September 2021.

Above: This time we see 43321 (formerly 43121) approaching Parson Street, just west of Bristol Temple Meads, with 1V50, the 06.06 Edinburgh to Plymouth. 5 January 2018.

Right: With people enjoying the seaside, 43357 is seen again, this time passing through Dawlish station with an unidentified southbound service. This is another view that is no longer the same, as the second phase of the sea wall rebuilding has now reached here during early 2022, changing the view to the right of the picture with a totally rebuilt platform and new raised wall. 24 August 2019.

Looking in the other direction from the station footbridge at Dawlish on the same day as the previous shot, this is 43321 rushing through with 1S51, the 12.27 Plymouth to Edinburgh service. 24 August 2019.

Above: From high above Marine Parade, we can see another busy day on the beach as 43303 (formerly 43103) passes through Dawlish station with a southbound service bound for Plymouth. 26 June 2010.

Left: Taken from the delightfully named Crooked Lane, this is 43366 (formerly 43166) passing near Brent Knoll on the Taunton to Bristol line with an unidentified northbound service. Since this image was taken, the location has inevitably become very overgrown, so this view is lost. 5 June 2010.

This time we are just south of Wickwar Tunnel, between Bristol and Gloucester, as 43303 has just exited with another southbound service heading for Plymouth. 5 September 2009.

43366 is captured drifting down the gradient through Lawrence Hill, just north of Bristol Temple Meads, with 1V50, the 06.06 Edinburgh to Plymouth service. The bridge above the train once carried the former Midland line from Bristol to the north; closed many years ago, it is now a footpath and cycleway. Since this image was taken, the double track line that originally ran beneath the bridge to the right of the picture has now been reinstated, returning this busy section from Bristol to Filton Abbey Wood back to four tracks once again. 13 January 2012.

This is the first of six images showing CrossCountry services off their normal operating routes. 43357 (formerly 43157) is captured passing Fairwood Junction, just west of Westbury and taking the station line with 1S51, the 11.53 Totnes to Edinburgh service, diverted due to planned engineering work in the Bristol area and also starting short of Plymouth for some reason. Western Region HSTs were an everyday sight here until their withdrawal from frontline services during 2019. 3 September 2021.

Still at Fairwood Junction on the same day but looking in the opposite direction to the previous image, this is the other latest addition to the CrossCountry fleet, former LNER power car 43208 heading west with 1V44, the 06.11 Leeds to Totnes service. 3 September 2021.

This time we see an even rarer location for a CrossCountry HST. This is 43378 at Swindon with an unidentified northbound service. The train had arrived via Bristol and reversed here, taking the Golden Valley route to Gloucester and the north. 43178 was originally allocated to the Western Region from new back in 1977, so it was briefly back on familiar territory! 1 November 2018.

Another diverted service is seen approaching Bradford-on-Avon headed by 43301 and bound for Plymouth. This location is sometimes known locally as 'The Avenue' due to the lines of huge conifer trees either side of the track and was a favourite spot for the well-known photographer Ivo Peters back in the 1950s and 1960s. 16 March 2019.

On a day of showers and with a nice patch of snowdrops in the station garden to the left, this is 43303 passing through Bradford-on-Avon station, with its nicely restored GWR seats and running in nameboard, with 1V44, the 05.18 Leeds to Exeter St Davids. CrossCountry services were being diverted via Westbury at this time due to flooding of the railway between Bridgwater and Taunton. 19 February 2014.

To round off the images of diversions, we see 43303 again, this time at Cole, just west of Bruton station, with 1V44, the 06.11 Leeds to Plymouth service. This image was taken from the embankment of the former Somerset & Dorset line, which crossed the Great Western Main Line here until closure of the S&D in 1966. 14 August 2021.

Back on more usual territory now as 43239 (formerly 43039) races west through Dawlish Warren with 1V44, the 06.11 Leeds to Plymouth once again. As mentioned earlier, this was one of the two extra power cars taken on by CrossCountry after they were removed from service by LNER in late 2019. 29 May 2021.

43304 (formerly 43104) passes through Teignmouth with a service bound for Plymouth. 43104 spent quite some time in storage and became quite a wreck during the late 1990s to early 2000s and at one point it was actually on the verge of scrapping. It was finally refurbished for Virgin XC as a replacement for 43029 that was transferred to Great Western during 2001. 29 August 2021.

Displaying a rather novel use for a former platform trolley at Newton Abbot station, this is 43301 on the rear of 1V44, the 06.11 Leeds to Plymouth. 10 July 2014.

After a few months of erratic use at the end of 2021 and into early 2022 due to crewing issues, sometimes only being used on Sundays, it is good to see sets have now returned to more usual service. 43304 is seen having just arrived at Plymouth on the rear of 1V44, the 06.11 from Leeds, while 43303 departs on the rear of 1M49, the 11.53 Plymouth to Birmingham New Street. 4 February 2022.

The station footbridge can be seen in the distance as 43384 (formerly 43184) races through the pointwork that leads into the down loop line at Yatton with 1V44, the 06.11 from Leeds to Plymouth. 43184 was another power car originally allocated to the Western Region when new. 5 April 2013.

Much further north at North Staffs Junction, just to the south of Derby, 43303 is heading south with 1V50, the 06.06 Edinburgh to Plymouth service. The area to the right of the picture was once the huge Willington Power Station complex that was fed by a continuous flow of merry-go-round coal trains up until its decommissioning and closure in the late 1990s. The lines above the train lead to Uttoxeter and Stoke-on-Trent. 11 February 2016.

Taken from a foot crossing just west of Tiverton Parkway, 43378 is leading 1V44, the 06.11 Leeds to Plymouth. 17 January 2019.

The white stuff is not a common sight in Devon! This, however, is 43304 drawing to a halt at a snowy Tiverton Parkway with 1S51, the 12.27 Plymouth to Edinburgh. 23 January 2013.

Left: 43207 (formerly 43007) is seen on the rear of 1S51, the 12.27 Plymouth to Edinburgh service making the call at Taunton station. 43007 was another power car first allocated to the Western Region way back in 1976. 1 October 2021.

Below: A fabulous summer's day sees 43357 (formerly 43157) approaching Whiteball Tunnel, between Exeter and Taunton, with a Plymouth to Edinburgh service. 26 June 2010.

The footbridge that was erected at Powderham during the mid-2010s to replace the rather hazardous foot crossing that had existed here previously has provided a fine grandstand for viewing passing trains. The city of Exeter and Exeter Cathedral can just be made out in the distance as 43304 approaches with a late-running Edinburgh to Plymouth service. 30 August 2019.

Right: No pot of gold at the end of this rainbow, just 43304 departing Taunton on the rear of 1V44, the 06.11 Leeds to Plymouth service. The rather messy area to the left is now a relief road. 10 December 2014.

Below: Taken on the same day as the previous image, this is 43304 passing over the flood channel on the approach to Exeter St Davids with 1S51, the 12.27 Plymouth to Edinburgh service. 10 December 2014.

The sea is in angry mood at Dawlish as 43378 passes by Marine Parade on a bright morning with 1V44, the 06.11 Leeds to Plymouth. Although this view is still available, it is far more hindered by the height of the new wall and fence to the right; the preliminary works had just started at this time with an excavator in place in the distance. 20 September 2019.

Recent vegetation clearance around the cliff top afforded this much higher viewpoint than the previous image of 43207 heading west with 1V44, the 06.11 Leeds to Plymouth service. Note also that by this time, the first few panels of concrete had been put in place for the sea wall reinforcements, which have since been completed. 18 February 2020.

43366 pulls away from the Exeter St Davids stop with 1V52, the 06.01 Glasgow Central to Paignton service. 24 August 2019.

On a very blustery and showery day and under some menacing looking clouds, 43378 passes the classic location of the skew bridge at Teignmouth with a Plymouth to Edinburgh service. 11 February 2011.

Chapter 5

Great Western Railway

A s many Great Western services were covered in my earlier book *HSTs: The Western Region*, I have only included a few of the present day GWR operations with Castle services to bring the story up to date so far.

Former celebrity power car 43172 is seen passing through Dawlish Warren with an Exeter St Davids to Penzance service. Up until September 2020, this example was in a one-off livery and named *Harry Patch The Last Survivor of The Trenches*. 29 May 2021.

Left: This is 43029 passing through Dawlish Warren with a Penzance to Exeter St Davids train, the preceding service to the one in the previous image. 29 May 2021.

Below: Taken from the well-known Langstone Rock, just west of Dawlish Warren, this is 43016 leading 2U12, the 06.40 Penzance to Cardiff Central service. This power car has recently been named *Powderham Castle*. 29 May 2021.

In a patch of weak winter morning sunshine, 43005 *St Michael's Mount* is arriving at Plymouth with 2U16, the 08.50 Penzance to Cardiff Central service. 4 February 2022.

This time we see 43194 *Okehampton Castle* leading 2C67, the 08.00 Cardiff Central to Penzance, past Sprey Point on the approach to Teignmouth on a lovely autumn morning. 43093 *Old Oak Common HST Depot 1976-2018* can be seen on the rear. 1 October 2021.

Above: Also seen at Sprey Point but heading in the other direction, this is 43027 leading 2U14, the 09.47 Plymouth to Cardiff Central. 43027 has been allocated to the Western Region ever since it was new back in 1977. 29 August 2021.

Left: Another lifelong Western Region example is 43010 seen arriving at Plymouth with 2C67, the 08.00 Cardiff Central to Penzance. 4 February 2022.

With the holidaymakers taking advantage of the late summer sunshine in time honoured fashion, 43040 passes by near Sprey Point, Teignmouth, with an Exeter St Davids to Penzance service. 29 August 2021.

With its unique mural commemorating Old Oak Common Depot, this is 43093 *Old Oak Common HST Depot 1976-2018* approaching Dawlish Warren with a Penzance to Exeter St Davids service. 29 May 2021.

43010 is seen again, this time arriving at Newport with 2U12, the 06.40 Penzance to Cardiff Central. 23 November 2021.

Chapter 6

Network Rail

The New Measurement Train (NMT) was created in response to the October 2000 Hatfield crash, which was deemed to be caused by something called gauge corner cracking on the running rails. Three power cars were initially obtained by Network Rail, 43013/014/062 all formerly with Virgin XC. Various coaching stock was assembled and formed up with the train making its debut in May 2003. Since that time, the 'Flying Banana', as it is often called, has covered many millions of miles on most major lines and some other secondary routes at regular intervals to detect various faults that may be present. A few of these services operating in the south of England are seen in this section.

Left: The first of three images taken on the same day show the NMT making its first visit to Bournemouth for Network Rail. This is 43062 *John Armitt* on the rear of 1X21, the 03.59 Old Oak Common to Reading via Bournemouth and Salisbury. 11 October 2007.

Below: Next, we see the train approaching Southampton Central where it will change direction with 43062 *John Armitt* now leading. 11 October 2007.

The huge nameboard leaves one in no doubt that the train has now arrived at Salisbury with 43013 leading, having reversed direction at Southampton Central. After a short layover here, the set then returned to London via Basingstoke and Reading. 11 October 2007.

Right: On one of the first times the NMT worked south of Bournemouth, this is 43013 leading 1Z23, the 14.52 Basingstoke to Old Oak Common via Weymouth, Basingstoke and Reading. This route is no longer on the NMT itinerary for some reason. 22 April 2010.

Below: During the first couple of years the NMT was operating, this particular power car was only used a few times while the three power cars mentioned in the introduction were overhauled so, despite being a pretty dull image, it is included for scarcity. 43154 is seen arriving at Taunton with a service that originated at Old Oak Common. It is now currently in service with GWR and named *Compton Castle*. 30 September 2005.

During most of the 2010s, 43013/014/062 were the only power cars used with the NMT but later in this decade, many more examples became available due to TOCs modernising their rolling stock. This is ex-LNER 43299 standing at Gillingham with 1Q23, the 05.56 Reading to Salisbury via Yeovil Junction and Exeter St Davids monthly circuit. 6 May 2021.

Just a month after the previous image and this is 43290 arriving at Gillingham with the same 1Q23, the 05.56 Reading to Salisbury. After well over 40 years in service, this was almost certainly the first time it had ever visited this location! 3 June 2021.

Three more images taken on the same day on another route not now covered by the NMT from Castle Cary to Weymouth. This is 1Q23, the 04.55 Old Oak Common to Weymouth via Basingstoke, Salisbury, Exeter, Westbury and Yeovil, arriving at Yeovil Pen Mill after the trip up the line from Exeter St Davids with 43062 *John Armitt* leading. 28 April 2011.

Standing in the unusual double-sided platform at Yeovil Pen Mill, this is 43013 on the rear of the train in the previous shot. 28 April 2011.

After reversing direction at Yeovil Pen Mill, this is 43013 now leading on the approach to Maiden Newton with the same train again. Although the West of England line from Salisbury to Exeter is still covered by the NMT these days, the trip to Weymouth from Yeovil on the return from Exeter no longer happens. Behind the bushes to the left of this image was the commencement of the former branch line to Bridport, closed in 1975 and now a public footpath. 28 April 2011.

Another section of line that does still see NMT activity is between Salisbury and Southampton, covered by an extension of the usual run to Exeter St Davids becoming 1X23, the 15.13 Salisbury to Salisbury via Southampton Central. The train is seen passing Millbrook Freightliner terminal headed by 43014 *The Railway Observer*. 19 June 2014.

This is the return of the train seen in the previous shot, again passing Millbrook and now with 43062 *John Armitt* leading. Both of these shots are no longer possible since the removal of the footbridge during late 2020. 19 June 2014.

Left: 1X23, the 15.13 Salisbury to Salisbury via Southampton is seen again, this time approaching Redbridge off the line from Romsey headed by 43062 *John Armitt*. 22 March 2012.

Below: Five years later and a final shot of 1X23 sees the train passing through Redbridge and beneath the bridge that the previous image was taken from as it heads back to Salisbury from Southampton Central. 9 March 2017.

Above: We now head west again as 43013 is captured on the rear of 1Q23, the Old Oak Common to Salisbury via Exeter St Davids as it passes just east of Tisbury on its way back from Exeter. 24 March 2011.

Right: Now for a couple of shots on the westerly end of the Salisbury to Exeter line in Devon as we see 43062 *John Armitt* passing through the newly double-tracked and re-instated up platform at Axminster station with 1Q23, the Old Oak Common to Salisbury via Exeter St Davids returning from Exeter. This is now a bi-directionally signalled section of line (known as a dynamic loop) which means the train is seen actually travelling over the down line in the up direction! 21 January 2010.

Further west still and we see 43014 departing from Exeter Central with 1Q23, the Old Oak Common to Salisbury via Exeter St Davids heading back to Salisbury. If one were stood on this bridge back in the line's heyday of the 1950s and 1960s, all you could see would have been a maze of tracks, rolling stock everywhere and a huge signal box behind the power car, all now vanished since the massive rationalisation that occurred here just over 50 years ago. 24 March 2011.

Mark Carne CBE

Above: Still on the West of England line but back in North Dorset, we see 43013 *Mark Carne CBE* running downhill towards Gillingham from Buckhorn Weston Tunnel with 1Q23, the 05.41 Reading Triangle Sidings to Salisbury via Exeter St Davids. Note that since the closure of Old Oak Common in the late 2010s, the start point for this regular train has changed. 20 September 2018.

Left: Gillingham signal box had only another year in service as 43062 *John Armitt* arrives with 1Q23, the Old Oak Common to Salisbury via Exeter St Davids returning to Salisbury. 21 January 2010.

Prior to 1966 this was a double track main line, believe it or not! 43062 *John Armitt* is seen again as it climbs the gradient up from Gillingham to pass beneath the overbridge at Motcombe, about a mile or so to the east. Back in the days of steam, this was quite a challenging gradient from Gillingham for about five miles or so to Semley, especially if the train had stopped at Gillingham station. 11 March 2021.

Above: This is 43013 passing Marine Parade on the approach to Dawlish with 1Q18, the 05.01 Old Oak Common to Old Oak Common via Plymouth. The new wall here comes up to just under the window line of the coaches but also has a fence on top of it, effectively ruining a shot such as this! 28 August 2015.

Right: This is the fine view to be had from the footbridge at Powderham, just east of Starcross, as 43062 *John Armitt* leads 1Z18, the 15.34 Paignton to Taunton. The train having earlier worked from Reading Triangle Sidings via Penzance to Paignton. 30 August 2019.

Although the NMT does have a regular run into South Wales, on this particular day it was running as a one-off. 43014 *The Railway Observer* is on the rear of the train crossing the River Usk at Newport with 1Q30, the 07.50 Crewe to Crewe via Newport. 24 February 2017.

Another operator to recently acquire power cars is Colas Rail, which hires them to Network Rail for test trains around the UK. One notable example is 43274, which was the only one ever to gain East Midlands Railway purple livery before it was taken out of use by the TOC. It has since gained Colas Rail logos on the bodysides and is seen here on the rear of 1Q23, the 05.56 Reading to Salisbury via Yeovil Junction and Exeter St Davids, at Gillingham on its return from Exeter. This was another example to be paying its first ever visit to this location. 18 November 2021.

Left: Things seem to move so quickly in railway circles these days. Newly acquired by Colas Rail, 43050 is seen approaching Heywood Village, just north of Westbury, with 1Z22, the 08.20 Tyseley to Bristol via Weymouth test train. This was one of the first times the power car was used but soon after this date, this one and 43060 on the rear were taken out of service in preference for MTU-engined examples. 4 November 2020.

Below: Quickly crossing to the other side of the bridge, this is 43060 bringing up the rear of the train in the previous image. 4 November 2020.

Chapter 7

Other Operators

A s power cars and stock became available over the years due to various operators modernising their fleets, other smaller operators saw that they still had potential as they were far from life expired. A few of these, past and present, are seen in this section to finish this volume.

Snapping up most of the buffer-fitted ex-Virgin XC power cars, Grand Central operated HST services on the ECML for around ten years or so during the mid-2000s to the mid-2010s and were painted in a distinctive black livery. This is 43067 arriving at York on a driver training run from King's Cross. 21 February 2008.

With quite a few people in the cab, this is 43080 on the other end of the train seen in the previous shot just about to depart south back to London. 21 February 2008.

This is the same driver training run from King's Cross as seen in the last image arriving into York on the previous day, this time with 43065 leading. 20 February 2008.

Towards the end of their time with Grand Central, the power cars received the new MTU engines like many others operators opted for and were renumbered to reflect this. The ones allocated to Grand Central all had '4' added after the class number. This is 43423 (formerly 43123) passing Doncaster with 1A61, the 08.42 Sunderland to London King's Cross service. The addition of the orange band really enhanced this livery. 23 September 2015.

Left: Heading in the other direction at Doncaster, this is 43465 (formerly 43065) heading 1N90, the 08.27 King's Cross to Sunderland service. 23 September 2015.

Below: Ex-East Midlands power cars 43059 and 43058 are seen passing through Eastleigh station, nearing the end of their journey with 0Z36, the 07.58 Crewe to Eastleigh Works for a repaint. 6 May 2021.

Two months after the previous shot was taken, 43059 with 43058 on the rear are absolutely spotless as they approach Shawford with 5Z64, the 13.35 Eastleigh Works to Crewe. These are now operated by Locomotive Services and during the summer of 2021 were used on the five-coach 'Staycation' services that ran over the Settle & Carlisle line. 12 July 2021.

Right: 43058 looks equally immaculate as it brings up the rear of 5Z64 passing through Shawford. 12 July 2021.

Below: Another power car to come under the Locomotive Services umbrella is InterCity-liveried 43049 *Neville Hill*. It is seen passing Shawford in the consist of 5Z44, the 11.10 Eastleigh Works to Crewe, hauled by 37521. It is interesting to compare this image with earlier ones in the Midland Main Line section. 30 March 2022.

Locomotive Services also operates a full nine-coach set as the Midland Pullman, which is painted in the livery of the original Blue Pullman diesel sets of the 1960s and is used for various tours throughout the UK. Making its first visit to the West Country, 43055 leads 1Z60, the 06.00 Eastleigh to Penzance, past Langstone Rock at Dawlish Warren. 29 May 2021.

To finish this volume are four images taken on the same day to bring the complicated story of HSTs up to date (so far at least!). Based in Germany, Rail Adventure is one of the latest operating companies to appear in the UK during 2021. It has secured eight power cars (although not all are intended for service), which are currently based at Eastleigh Works. During early 2022, test runs were carried out with 43465 and 43468 on the short section between Eastleigh and Fareham. This image shows the style of branding on the bodyside of 43468 stood at Fareham. 29 March 2022.

Just a couple of months later and this is 43046 *Geoff Drury 1930-1999 Steam Preservation and Computerised Track Recording Pioneer* leading 1Z50, the 06.36 Peterborough to Kingswear 'Devonian Pullman' charter through Bruton, Somerset. It was a daily occurrence to see HSTs passing here for over 40 years until 2019, but this was the first one in this area for two years following the withdrawal of the sets from frontline GWR services. 30 August 2021.

It is a far cry from the Grand Central livery previously carried by these examples! Note also that they do not carry a yellow-painted front end either. A wider view of 43468 at Fareham. 29 March 2022.

The immaculate pair are seen again at Fareham waiting to head back to Eastleigh. Around four or five out and back trips were made each day for two days. 29 March 2022.

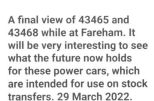

A final view of 43465 and 43468 while at Fareham. It will be very interesting to see what the future now holds for these power cars, which are intended for use on stock transfers. 29 March 2022.

Other books you might like:

Britain's Railways Series,
Vol. 12

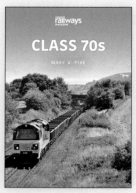

Britain's Railways Series,
Vol. 16

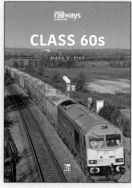

Britain's Railways Series,
Vol. 17

Britain's Railways Series,
Vol. 23

Britain's Railways Series,
Vol. 25

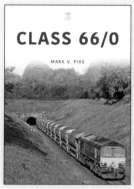

Britain's Railways Series,
Vol. 32

For our full range of titles please visit:
shop.keypublishing.com/books

VIP Book Club
Sign up today and receive
TWO FREE E-BOOKS

Be the first to find out about our forthcoming
book releases and receive exclusive offers.

Register now at keypublishing.com/vip-book-club

*Our VIP Book Club is a 100% spam-free zone, and we will never share your email with anyone else.
You can read our full privacy policy at: privacy.keypublishing.com*